Hamilcar Barca: The Life and Legacy of the Legendary Carthaginian General

By Charles River Editors

A modern depiction of Hannibal vowing revenge against Rome

Introduction

Alexander Van Loon's picture of Carthaginian armor from the 3rd century BCE

Carthage was one of the great ancient civilizations, and at its peak, the wealthy Carthaginian empire dominated the Mediterranean against the likes of Greece and Rome, with commercial enterprises and influence stretching from Spain to Turkey. In fact, at several points in history it had a very real chance of replacing the fledgling Roman empire or the failing Greek *poleis* (city-states) altogether as master of the Mediterranean. Although Carthage by far preferred to exert economic pressure and influence before resorting to direct military power (and even went so far as to rely primarily on mercenary armies paid with its vast wealth for much of its history, it nonetheless produced a number of outstanding generals, from the likes of Hanno Magnus to, of course, the great bogeyman of Roman nightmares himself: Hannibal.

However, the Carthaginians' foreign policy had one fatal flaw - they had a knack over the centuries of picking the worst enemies to fight. The first serious clash of civilizations Carthage faced was against Greece, which rapidly became hostile when the Carthaginians began pushing to spread their influence towards the colonies known as *Magna Graecia* ("Great Greece"). Those colonies had been established in southern Italy and Sicily by several Greek *poleis*, and these territories would become a *casus belli* for the First Punic War.

Certain foreign policy decisions led to continuing enmity between Carthage and the burgeoning power of Rome, and what followed was a series of wars which turned from a battle for Mediterranean hegemony into an all-out struggle for survival. Although the Romans gained the upper hand in the wake of the First Punic War, the Carthaginians brought the Romans to their knees for over a decade during the Second Punic War. Of course, they were led in Italy by the legendary Hannibal Barca, who maintained his army near Rome for nearly 15 years, but never attempted to march on Rome.

One overlooked figure in the Punic Wars is Hamilcar Barca, who is now best remembered for being Hannibal's father. However, before Hannibal marched out of Spain, it was Hamilcar who had positioned forces there, and he was already a significant historical figure in his own right. Indeed, had it not been for his death, his legacy likely would have been more important than that of his illustrious son, who is now remembered as one of history's greatest generals.

Hamilcar Barca: The Life and Legacy of the Legendary Carthaginian General

The Founders

The Phoenicians are primarily known in the modern world for creating the oldest confirmed alphabet used as the basis for Arabic script, the Greek and Latin alphabets, and subsequent scripts developed from these. However, they were, for a significant period, also the most important commercial power in the Mediterranean world, responsible for founding a number of colonies, the most important being Carthage.

Contrary to claims made in the *Old Testament,* the Phoenicians were not sons of Ham but Canaanites.[1] They were a Semitic people speaking a Semitic language. They settled on a narrow strip of land between the mountains of Lebanon and the sea in what came to be known as Phoenicia. It was the Greeks who gave them the name of "Phoenicians" - meaning dark-skinned - and they were definitely not autochthonous. However, the specific date around which they arrived is still unknown.

Phoenicia was well-placed for trade as it lay halfway between the Hittites to the north and the Egyptians to the south, and it was a natural stopping-off point for the many caravan routes through which trade in the Middle East flowed. Lebanon was also blessed with a particularly important natural resource - cedar trees - ideal for ship-building. Phoenicia became the hub for trade in incense, myrrh, and onyx from Arabia, precious stones, spices, ivory, and perfumed wood from India, horse's linen and cotton from Egypt, gold, ebony, ivory, and slaves from Africa, and wheat and silver from Spain. In addition, Phoenician traders visited as far a-field as Austria and Germany, England, the Caucasus, as well as all neighboring Middle Eastern states.[2]

The Phoenicians also provided manufactured goods, and their factories turned out consumer goods in large quantities. Their Phoenician vases, jewels, necklaces, bracelets, brooches, images of the gods, and textiles, in particular, came to be highly prized. Their specialties were transparent glass made from the fine white sand found on the coast and Tyrian purple, a dye made from the murex, which provided the purple color unique to Phoenician mollusks.[3] Their builders were much sought after, and Phoenicians reputedly worked on Solomon's Temple in Jerusalem.[4] As well as building specific monuments, they were contracted to build ports and fleets, such as that of the king of the Neo-Assyrian Empire, Sennacherib of Assyria (c. 745-681 BCE), who entrusted them with the building of his Persian Gulf fleet.[5]

Such high volumes of trade necessitated the keeping of records, and the Phoenicians traded in writing materials, using papyrus from Egypt to replace clay tablets as the main material for recording transactions. Much of this trade in papyrus centered on the city of Byblos, and its name

---

[1] *Genesis*, VI; X, 15-16.
[2] Aubet, 2001
[3] *St. Clair, 2016*
[4] *1 Kings VII, 13-17.*
[5] *Frahm, 2017*

is where the word "book" derives from. However, it was the related development of the alphabet that proved the most historically significant, as this became the basis for the Hebrew, Greek, Etruscan, Latin, and Cyrillic alphabets.[6] Given this immense contribution to world literacy, it is devastating that all Phoenician literature has been lost to the modern world. Today, only the Maltese language retains some aspects of the original Phoenician language.

Significantly, there was no definitive Phoenician state. [7] Instead, there were numerous relatively small towns and cities spread along the coast, all more or less independent but united through their worship of the same gods. According to various Roman and Greek sources, Phoenicians (and later Carthaginians) sacrificed infants to their gods. Plutarch refers to the practice, as do others, including Tertullian, Plato, and Quintus Curtius Rufus.[8] Livy and Polybius, however, do not. While the bones of many infants have been found in Carthaginian archaeological sites, their cause of death remains a topic of fierce debate.[9] In a child cemetery called the *Tophet* - the word means "roasting place" - an estimated 20,000 urns have been uncovered.[10] The Bible asserts that children were sacrificed at the tophet to the god Moloch.[11]

According to Diodorus Siculus's *Bibliotheca historica,* "There was in their city a bronze image of Cronus extending its hands, palms up and sloping toward the ground, so that each of the children when placed thereon rolled down and fell into a sort of gaping pit filled with fire."[12] Plutarch, however, argued that the children were already dead at the time, having been killed by their parents or with their permission.[13] Modern academics are divided over the issue of infant sacrifice, and there is a growing opinion that the claim was, in fact, a deliberate propaganda invention of the Romans to discredit their enemies.[14]

The sites of Phoenician settlements were all very similar, either on islands close to the coast with good anchorage, such as Tyre, or on headlands with a good anchorage that was easier to defend, such as Byblos and Sidon. At various times in history, the Phoenicians came under the sway of larger powers, such as the Egyptians and the Hittites, but nonetheless, through their favorable geographic position, they were still able to develop their trade, largely through founding settlements overseas.[15] Some were essentially concessions, as in Memphis in Egypt, while others were trading stations, some of which then went on to become colonies that expanded into surrounding areas, such as Carthage. Phoenician settlements have been found in

---

[6] *Coulmas, 1996; Roger, 2004*

[7] "Heilbrunn," 2000

[8] Plutarch, Moralia II.171C; Tertullian, *Apology* IX.2-3; Plato, Minos, 315; Quintus Curtius Rufus, *History of Alexander* IV.III.23.

[9] Higgins, 2005

[10] "Relics," 1987

[11] *Jeremiah*, VII:30-32; *2 Kings*, XXIII.10 & XVII.17.

[12] Diodorus Siculus, *Bibliotheca historica*, XX.1.4.

[13] Plutarch, *Moralia 2, De Superstitione* 3.

[14] Fantar, 2000

[15] *Stieglitz, 1990*

Cyprus, Crete, and throughout Asia Minor. At Gades (modern-day Cadiz), archaeologists have dated its foundations to as early as 1100 BCE. Trading stations have also been unearthed in Sardinia, Malta, Gozo, Pantelleria, Sicily, and Ibiza.

The Mediterranean Rivalry

Carthage was almost certainly founded during the colonization boom of the Phoenician Empire. This was a movement which took advantage of the relative collapse in the fortunes of Greece, Crete and the Hittite Empire to establish a string of up to 3,000 colonies between Asia Minor and Spain, and Carthage was conveniently positioned smack in the middle of the extremely lucrative Iberia–Asia Minor raw metals route. Although it was a convenient position, Carthage itself was apparently not intended to be anything special in terms of colonizing efforts, particularly because the Phoenician colonial method differed radically from the Greek variant. While the Hellenes would create a settlement that was self-sustaining and almost always self-governing, while still retaining ties of alliance and friendship with the so-called "Mother City" on mainland Greece, the Phoenicians, both for administrative control reasons and due to population constraints, did not as a rule create self-sufficient colonies. Instead, the Phoenicians exerted more control over the settlements, particularly when it came to trade regulations. Thus, the settlement which gradually spread upon the hill of Byrsa was very low in the food chain.

From 850–650 BCE, Carthage gradually became more and more wealthy thanks to her privileged position straddling the major land and sea trade routes of the Mediterranean. These two centuries saw the emergence of what would later become known as "Punic" (Carthaginian) culture, a distinctly West African Phoenician identity which differed noticeably from its predecessor. The growth of this culture indicated a rise in influence on Carthage's part, and that rise manifested itself in 650 BCE when Carthage founded its own independent colony, a settlement on Ibiza, without assistance from Tyre. As the fortunes of Tyre and the Phoenician Empire waned, first with the loss of Sicily to the ever-expanding Greeks and then with Nebuchadnezzar of Babylon's great siege of Tyre in 585 BCE, Carthage's fortunes continued to rise. More settlements were founded, more cities of the North African seaboard were brought under direct Carthaginian control rather than paying their dues to Tyre, and a large colony was established in Syrtis, between Tunisia and Lybia. Additionally, Carthage's rise was bolstered by the influx of a large number of immigrants of both wealth and high political status from Tyre itself, as many of the elite fled the conflicts which enveloped the Phoenician capital.

For centuries, Carthage's expansion had progressed relatively smoothly, with no one challenging their dominion over the Mediterranean. Even the Etruscans, whose heyday coincided with Carthage's rise to prominence, had not vied with the Punic Empire for supremacy. In fact, the Etruscans had become valued trading partners and then allies, despite several incidents involving pirates.

However, near the end of the 6th century, a new power was emerging on the Mediterranean with hitherto unseen forcefulness, swallowing up the Etruscan cities and pursuing a policy of ruthless military expansion which threatened to upset the balance of power for good. The Carthaginian elite felt nervous enough watching the rapid growth of Rome that in 509 BCE, a treaty, the first of several, was signed between Carthage and Rome. Although at the time Carthage was far more significant both politically and militarily, an ally on the Italian mainland who would be both belligerent and at odds with the Greeks was certainly useful. The treaty itself was similar to others that the Carthaginians had signed with various states throughout the Mediterranean, and it served to limit the sphere of influence and commercial enterprise each power was meant to abide by.

In 348 BCE, Carthage signed another treaty with Rome, which was now quickly becoming the dominant power in Italy. Rome gained trade access (but not settlement rights) to Sicily, while Carthage maintained a monopoly on trade in Iberia and Sardinia. Rome also gained valuable Latin possessions from the treaty, further cementing its position as a dominant Italian power.

This initially cordial relationship, however, would prove to be far from lasting. Inevitably, Carthage and Rome would be locked in a mortal struggle that would define one city and ruin the other.

Sicily was largely at peace, barring the occasional skirmish, for several decades after the peace with Agathocles, but Carthage had plenty of internal and external threats to worry about, not least the burgeoning power of Rome, despite their peace treaty (another treaty was allegedly signed in 306 BC, but its authenticity is questionable). Sicily was not a problem again until around 280, when Carthage launched a renewed attack on the Sicilian city-states, seizing Akragas and besieging Syracuse. Pyrrhus, King of Epirus, was busy waging war against the Roman Republic in Southern Italy when he received a request for aid from several Sicilian *poleis*, Syracuse among them, against Carthage.

Ancient bust of Pyrrhus

Pyrrhus sailed for Sicily with a vast army, forcing Mago, the Carthaginian general, to lift the siege of Syracuse. Pyrrhus then captured Eryx and demanded that Carthage quit the island of Sicily entirely. When these terms were refused, he once again defeated the Carthaginian army in the field in 276. However, Pyrrhus, able general though he was, had made himself increasingly unpopular among the Sicilian *poleis* both for his blatant power grabbing and for his cavalier treatment of allies, so much so that he was forced to depart from Sicily. Pyrrhus's fleet suffered a heavy defeat at sea at the hands of the Carthaginian navy, and he would go on to a crippling campaign in southern Italy which eventually resulted in Rome absorbing virtually the entire lower half of the Italian peninsula into its own domains, bringing its borders onto Carthage's Sicilian doorstep. Something had to give.

After a period of increased tension, the inevitable war finally erupted in 264 BCE. With the domination of many of the city states, and with only Syracuse the true threat, the Carthaginians decided that they had invested far too much money, time, and effort in their war against the Greek city states to simply abandon the field. Carthage, with its eyes firmly resting upon a future ripe with financial possibilities as well as the ability to allow Carthaginian colonization, settled in for the long haul. Shortly after the decision was made to continue the effort, though, the ruler of Syracuse died, and as far as the Carthaginians knew the resistance had ended.

This was not the case. A group of Italian mercenaries who had been hired by the city of Syracuse started to make their way back to Italy when they stopped in the city of Messana, which offered them rest and hospitality before continuing their journey. The mercenaries took advantage of the situation and "treacherously seized Messana…they expelled or slew the male inhabitants, divided their wives and children" (Smith, The Punic Wars, 3) and took control of the city. These mercenaries decided to call themselves "the children of Mamers, or Mars" (Smith, The Punic Wars, 3) and sought to establish themselves as a power. Carthage disagreed with that plan.

When Carthage learned of the treachery of the mercenaries, they started to march upon the city of Messana. It was the Carthaginians' intent to punish and capture those mercenaries that they could. The mercenaries, upon discovering that they were now in the path of Carthage's fury, found their courage wanting. The mercenaries decided to "petition Rome to intercede" upon their behalf. The mercenaries reminded the Roman Senate in their plea that the mercenaries were Italians and that it was the responsibility and duty of Rome to come to their aid. To leave the mercenaries to the fate which Carthage was going to dictate would show that Rome had no power over Sicily, and that, more importantly, Rome was ignoring its responsibilities to watch out for its Latin brethren.

For its part, Carthage was not concerned with any plea that the mercenaries made. Carthage believed that the treachery of the mercenaries, so foreign to the rigorous decorum and high moral standards of the Roman culture, would prohibit the Roman Senate from voting to send any sort of assistance to the mercenaries.

However, Rome's reasons for fighting the First Punic War were as clear cut as Carthage's. Rome sought to not only protect its own holdings in Sicily (as well as their allies), they were also concerned about either the Greeks or the Carthaginians increasing their strength on the island. Such a buildup of strength would directly affect the safety of Rome itself.

In addition to protecting itself Rome also had economic reasons. Obtaining more influence on Sicily would increase trade and the ability to export materials to new markets. City states defeated would not only be allied to Rome but some of the conquered states' lands would be doled out to worthy Roman citizens.

Thus, when the Italians who had seized Messana sent a delegation to the Roman Senate seeking assistance, the Roman Senate could not "refuse to protect Italians who appealed to them avowedly as the head of the Italian confederation for aid against the Greeks and Carthaginians" (Smith, The Punic Wars, 5). The Roman Senate, honor bound, could not "look calmly on while the city of Messana fell into the hands of the Carthaginians." (Smith, The Punic Wars, 5).

Understanding these needs, the Roman consuls found that they were able "to raise a patriotic cry of Italians against foreigners." (Smith, The Punic Wars, 6). With this public backing, the Roman government could successfully prepare the state for war against Carthage.

In addition to the requirements of Roman honor, there was the basic necessity to maintain the protective barrier around the city of Rome. The Roman Senate understood that the city of Messana could be used by the Carthaginians "as a standing menace to their [Roman] power and a vantage ground in the great conflict." (Smith, The Punic Wars, 5). The Roman government was quite sure this would be the case in the near future.

It was against this backdrop that Hamilcar Barca would become one of Carthage's most important leaders.

The Barca Dynasty

Originally, Carthage was a monarchy, but by the 5th century BCE, it had a form of government not dissimilar to that of Republican Rome. It had *Suffetes* as chief magistrates rather than Consuls, a Senate, and an Assembly, and a Board of Judges was formed after an unsuccessful military coup to control army commanders.[16] Around the same time as the introduction of the Board of Judges, the policy of relying on mercenaries rather than troops raised from the population was introduced. The exception was the Sacred Band, a unit akin to the Praetorian Guard made up of Carthaginian aristocrats. Aristotle analyzed the constitution of Carthage and seemed impressed by what he observed - the choice of leaders depended on eminence rather than age, and those co-opted into office served for lengthy periods.[17] Indeed, those in office should be not only the most efficient but also the wealthiest, and Aristotle argued that only the rich could be good rulers and have the time to devote to their duties. Of course, this seems to ignore the fact that the Carthaginian system lent itself to corruption, where the highest offices were for sale, and those who bought power inevitably demanded a return on their investment.

Hamilcar hailed from a family jockeying for power within this structure, and the absence of Carthaginian sources and a general scarcity of information regarding the background of the Barca family has ensured that the origins of the powerful dynasty have attracted scholarly interest recently. Plenty of the attention has concentrated on the actual origin of the name "Barca" itself. Some suggestions state it comes from the city of Barce, a Cyrenaic city, while others conclude that since Hamilcar was the first notable historical figure to have the name Barca, it could have been a nickname (meaning "lightning" in his case). The rationale behind this conclusion is that the name derives from the Phoenician word *brqand*, equivalent to the Greek epithet *keraunos*, although there is an absence of primary sources referencing this idea. That said, the fact that the name Barca was passed on to Hamilcar's sons indicates it was likely a

---

¹⁶ Livy, *History of Rome,* XXX.7.5; Bondi, 2001
¹⁷ *Aristotle, Politics: A Treatise on Government.*

family name. As for his first name, Hamilcar is the Latinization of "Hamílkas," the Hellenized form of the common Semitic Phoenician-Carthaginian masculine given name *ḤMLK*, meaning "Melqart's brother."[18]

Hamilcar's family is thought to have come from Cyrenaica, possibly settling in Carthage as late as the 3rd century BCE.[19] Textual evidence coming from Polybius and Diodorus[20] could explain the family's apparent animosity toward the Carthaginian Council of Elders and their departure to Spain. What is certainly known is that the Barcid family was well-established in Carthage by the 3rd century BCE, and they were one of the leading families in the city's ruling oligarchy, coming to prominence during the First Punic War (264–241 BCE), largely due to their open hostility towards Rome. They argued that the rising new power of Rome constituted a serious threat to Carthage's mercantile power, and that Rome had to be confronted and contained at all costs.

Hamilcar Barca lived from 275-228 BCE and served as a Carthaginian general in both the First Punic War and the subsequent Mercenary War (240 BCE–238 BCE). The known members of his family included his eldest son, Hannibal, one of the most famous generals in history.[21] The name of Hamilcar's wife is unknown, but together, they had six children, including three sons - Hannibal, Hasdrubal, and Mago - each of which became famous military leaders in their own right. Their three daughters married Barcid family allies. His eldest daughter's name is also unknown, but she married Bomilcar and became the mother of Hanno the Explorer.[22] Another daughter married Hasdrubal the Fair (270 BCE–221 BCE).[23] His youngest daughter, supposedly named Salammbo, married Naravas, a Numidian chieftain.

Hamilcar's personal rise would be directly linked to his actions and leadership in the First Punic War.

The First Punic War

In the First Punic War, as in previous conflicts, Carthage had relied upon the hiring of mercenary troops. These troops, coming from all around the Mediterranean and specializing in a wide array of weapons and tactics, were commanded by their own native officers. The various mercenary units, however, were under the command of a professional Carthaginian soldier. On Sicily, the Carthaginians had landed their mercenary units, but never together or with a clearly designed or coordinated plan of attack.

The Battle of Agrigentum also caused a shift in policy among the Carthaginian military elite.

---

[18] Lancel, 1999

[19] Bath, 1995

[20] Polybius, *Histories,* I; Diodorus, *Bibliotheca historica,* XXV.

[21] Hoyos, 2008

[22] Although Law describes Hanno as Hamilcar's son, rather than his grandson (1978, p. 121).

[23] Livy, *History of Rome,* XXI.2.

Rather than face the legions on land, they would attempt to resolve the conflict at sea, where their massive and highly proficient professional navy had the advantage.

That said, with few positions of strength remaining to them on the island, the Carthaginian forces under the command of the Carthaginian Hamilcar Barca opted to attack Italy. By using the Carthaginian navy and its skill upon the seas, Hamilcar launched a series of raids along the Italian coast in an effort to bring the war home to the Romans and to force Rome to withdraw its forces from Sicily. Rome did not withdraw, however, nor did it relinquish any territory which it had gained. Instead, it held firmly onto the conquests they had made on land.

That said, by 260 BCE it was clear that the war's focus would switch to the sea. Indeed, as it would turn out, the "decisive actions in the First Punic War were on the seas." (US Army Command and General Staff College, *Force Projection in the Punic Wars*, 3). For Rome, the First Punic War was the beginning of its martial navy; while Rome had sailors who were fairly adept at plying the trade routes through the Mediterranean, they didn't enjoy any sort of maritime prowess in regards to warfare upon the sea. Upon the outbreak of war with Carthage, however, this all changed. The Carthaginians were the undeniable superpower on the Mediterranean and had been for centuries; they could, quite literally, sail circles around the Roman navy at the beginning of the war. The Romans, however, were quick learners, something the Carthaginians discovered to their detriment, and the First Punic War saw the "largest naval engagements until the 20th century." (US Army Command and General Staff College, *Force Projection in the Punic Wars*, 9).

At the beginning of the war, the Carthaginian navy, manned by native Carthaginians and not mercenaries, were fully capable of defeating the few ships which the Romans were able to launch. The Carthaginian navy was also able to force the Roman troopships off of their marks, making them land farther from their intended destinations or forcing them to attempt night crossings, which were always dangerous even for the most skilled sailors. Rome, however, soon learned how to build ships equal to the Carthaginians' through the capture of the Carthaginian ship.

The Roman navy was dealt a crushing defeat at the Battle of Lipara, but Rome did not take this defeat lying down. Instead, the Senate authorized a massive financial package for the navy, boosting wartime production to hitherto untold (and virtually unsustainable) levels so that more than 100 Roman triremes were constructed within less than two months, a monumental undertaking. Once Rome had the ships, however, the Romans still needed to find experienced captains and crews to use those ships effectively, so a stopgap solution was developed: the *corvus*. Rather than ram the enemy ships and try to sink them, the Roman galleys would close alongside the Carthaginians and then drop the *corvus*, a hook-ended bridge, onto the enemy deck, linking the ships together. Once that was in place, Roman legionaries would swarm across the bridge, effectively turning a naval battle into a land one and returning the combat to terms which were favorable to them. The Carthaginians suffered grievously at the hands of this brilliantly simple device (though it was eventually phased out of service as the Roman navy became as adept as its Punic counterpart) and would gradually lose supremacy on the Mediterranean over the duration of the war.

By 257 BCE, Carthaginians had ceased their raids upon Italy, and a year later, the Romans decided to test their burgeoning naval skills once more in what would be known as the Battle of Cape Ecnomus, perhaps the largest naval battle in all of antiquity. Both fleets were of such immense size that each one had two separate commanders; for the Roman fleet, these commanders were the consuls Marcus Atalius Regulus and Lucius Manlius, while the Carthaginian commanders were Hanno and Hamilcar. Both Hanno and Hamilcar were battle tested commanders, while the consuls were elected officials.

The forces were evenly matched in spite of the Roman navy's relative youth and inexperience, and the battle was a long and fierce fight. Eventually, the Romans defeated the Carthaginians and drove them away from the Italian coast, taking hold of the ships abandoned by the Carthaginians and adding them to their fleet. With their victory at Ecnomus, Rome had successfully driven the war away from Italy and opened the path to North Africa, which would let them bring the war to the Carthaginians.

With the sea lanes to North Africa open, the Romans prepared an invasion force to assault the Carthaginian home territory, and in 255 they landed their legions in North Africa seeking to crush the Carthaginians. Naturally, the Carthaginians did not wait while Rome moved towards Carthage; the city's government sought out a commander for their mercenary army and chose a Spartan trained general, a Greek mercenary by the name of Xanthippos. The Carthaginians, changing their policy of keeping only a Carthaginian in the position of supreme command, hired Xanthippos and brought him to Carthage.

Once in the city, Xanthippos went amongst the mercenaries, some of whom he had fought with and others whom he had fought against. These mercenaries knew the merits and victories of Xanthippos and gave him a measure of respect that no Carthaginian could hope to command, and this respect translated to rapid responses to his orders.

This helped bring about the crucial Carthaginian victory in the battle of Tunis in 255. At that battle, nearly half of the Roman army and the consul Regulus were captured by Xanthippos' troops. The surviving legionaries, about 5,000 men, dug into a position which they could easily defend, and shortly after the battle, the remaining Roman troops were rescued by a portion of the Roman fleet. The Roman defeat at the hands of Xanthippos marked the end of Roman efforts in North Africa.

By 254, the Carthaginian army returned to Sicily in an effort to take back their lost holdings and to seize the entire island. At the same time, Carthage made the decision to release

Xanthippos, so in 251, Hasdrubal was the commander of the Carthaginian forces on Sicily. In the northwest of Sicily, the Roman and Carthaginian forces met in the battle of Panormus, and Hasdrubal's troops were defeated and pushed back, eliciting an attempt at peace negotiations from the Carthaginians. This gesture was made through the release of the consul Regulus who had been captured at the battle of Tunis.

Hamilcar took sole command of Carthaginian land forces in Sicily in 247 BCE, and for the next six years, he kept his army intact and led a successful guerrilla war against the Romans. When Hamilcar first arrived in Sicily, the Carthaginians had temporarily regained control of the seas, but on land, they only held the cities of Lilybaeum and Drepanum. He was somewhat hampered by the internal wranglings of the ruling aristocracy as to where Carthaginian resources should be focused. Those favoring an expansionist policy in North Africa, led by Hanno II (who was also pro-Rome), won out over those who favored Hamilcar's option for using their restored naval dominance to retake the areas of Sicily they had lost and then took the war into Italy. The rivalry for control of Carthage's foreign policy between Hanno's aristocratic "Peace Party" and Hamilcar's supporters, mainly the merchant class and ordinary citizens, would shape Carthaginian politics for years to come.

At the time, Carthage found it hard to sustain the war on its two major fronts. In addition to maintaining a fleet and an army in Sicily, they had to deal with Libyans and Numidians in northern Africa. The lack of resources to deal with both threats meant Hamilcar was only given a small army to defend Sicily, and the Carthaginian fleet was gradually withdrawn. By 242 BCE, Carthage had virtually no naval presence left in Sicily.

Hamilcar based himself near Panormus in 247 BCE, at a time when many in Carthage believed there was no point in sending a large force to Sicily. With such a small force and no money with which to hire new troops, Hamilcar's strategic goal was basically limited to maintaining a stalemate. He was frustrated by the fact he had neither the means to prosecute the war, nor did he have the delegated authority to reach a peaceful settlement. The troops he did have were almost entirely mercenaries drawn from numerous nations. However, Hamilcar's leadership skills were first revealed in his ability to shape the unprepossessing collection into an effective fighting force, while his tactical genius proved invaluable in the war against the Romans in Sicily.[24]

Military strategists have long compared Hamilcar's employment of combined arms tactics to similar approaches used by Alexander the Great and Pyrrhus.[25] The difference is that Roman Commander Quintus Fabius Maximus had a much larger force than his adversary, no supply problems, and room to maneuvre, while Hamilcar was hemmed in, had a far smaller army than the Romans and was dependent on seaborne supplies from Carthage, which proved unreliable.

---

[24] Plutarch, *Parallel Lives: Life of Cato the Elder,* VIII.14.
[25] Ironically, the Romans used the same tactics in the Second Punic War against Hannibal.

Having arrived to find a dispirited and disgruntled army, Hamilcar's first task upon taking up command in the summer of 247 BCE was to deal with the rebellion of the mercenary troops, who were exasperated at Carthage's failure to pay them. Hamilcar took decisive action, murdering some of the ringleaders at night, drowning many others at sea, and dispersing more in different parts of North Africa.[26] Another major task was to enhance the spirit of the army in the process of creating a highly disciplined and versatile force. He built a bastion named Heircte near Panormus, from which he organized his guerrilla war against the Romans between 247 and 244 BCE

Hamilcar's occupation of the height of Heircte has been explored in a number of academic works,[27] with four possible locations being identified as the actual site of the fort. Hamilcar was said to have decided on his site when returning from a raid on the Italian coast. Its commanding position beside the sea made it the ideal spot, as there was also a sheltered bay at the foot of the mountain where he could build a naval station. Polybius recorded the site as being at or over Heircte between Eryx and by the sea at Panormus, and he described the mountain as "a steep height rising from the surrounding country to a considerable height. Of this the circumference of the top crest is not under a hundred stades. The site enclosed by which is well-pastured and cultivable, lying suitably protected against the sea-winds, quite spared from life-threatening animals."[28]

Both the sea side and the side looking inland had inaccessible cliffs, while the other sides needed only slight and limited preparation for an effective defense. A hillock served as a citadel and observation point "with the position commanding a convenient harbour for the trip from Drepana and Lilybaeum to Italy, in which there exists a plentiful supply of water."[29]

Hamilcar was not, however, content to sit in his impregnable fortress, and he began planning and carrying out raids to disrupt the Romans, going even beyond Sicily. For example, he raided Locri in Bruttium and the area around Brindisi in 247 BCE, and he also carried out seaborne raids ranging from Catana in Sicily to Cumae in central Italy. On the other hand, Hamilcar did not allow himself to be drawn into a large set-piece battle, so he won no major confrontation and recaptured no cities lost to the Romans during this period. Instead, he waged a relentless hit-and-run campaign that proved a constant drain on Roman resources.

A Roman army led by consuls Marcus Otacilius Crassus and Marcus Fabius Licinius failed against Hamilcar in 246 BCE, and the consuls in 245 BCE, Marcus Fabius Buteo and Atilius Bulbus, fared no better. In 244 BCE, Hamilcar moved his army to the slopes of Mount Eryx at night to provide support to the besieged garrison in the neighboring town of Drepana. He then retook the town of Eryx, which had been captured by the Romans in 249 BCE, and evacuated the

---

[26] Zonaras, *Annals of Rome*, VIII.16.
[27] Lazenby, 1996; Diodorus, XX.10.4; Pyrrhus, XXIII.20.
[28] Polybius, *Histories,* I.56.3-8.
[29] Polybius, *Histories,* I.56.3-8

population to Drepana.[30] Hamilcar continued his campaign from his new base for another two years. While Drepana kept him resupplied, by that time all Carthaginian ships had been recalled, so he was unable to launch any seaborne raids.

A well-known story of Hamilcar's attitude comes from a raid authorized by him but led by an officer named Bodostor. Hamilcar had given instructions that troops were not to plunder but simply attack, inflict damage, and retire quickly. Bodostor disobeyed his instructions, and his force was caught by the Romans, who inflicted heavy casualties on the Carthaginians. Hamilcar asked for a truce to bury the dead, but the Roman Consul Fundanius refused, saying that Hamilcar should request a truce to save the living. Hamilcar responded by attacking and inflicting severe casualties on the Romans. When Fundanius requested a truce to bury his dead in turn, Hamilcar replied that his quarrel was only with the living, and the dead had already settled their dues. He subsequently granted the truce.[31]

The Romans' inability to defeat Hamilcar or take the remaining Carthaginian-held cities resulted in their decision to construct a new fleet in 243 BCE and consolidate control of the sea and cut all of Hamilcar's links to home. Whether due to this new initiative or the constant raiding, Celtic mercenaries tried unsuccessfully to let the Romans into the Carthaginian base. Hamilcar had to promise huge rewards to keep the rest of his army loyal, but this tactic would later have severe repercussions.

By then, Rome was very nearly bankrupt and had to borrow from its wealthiest citizens to build a new fleet of 200 quinqueremes. The fleet enabled the Romans to seize the harbors at Drepana and Lilybaeum while Roman soldiers built siege works around Drepanum. The belated attempt by the Carthaginians to counter the Roman fleet failed at the Battle of the Aegates Islands in 241 BCE, a battle confirming and completing Sicily's isolation from Carthage.

From the Carthaginian perspective, the situation was untenable, and it was Hamilcar who was delegated to open negotiations with Roman Commander Gaius Lutatius Catulus. In turn, Hamilcar nominated Gisco, a Carthaginian commander of Lilybaeum, to lead the talks. Hamilcar's reluctance to put himself at the head of the negotiating team was arguably based on the fact that Carthage often brought defeated generals and admirals before the Tribunal of 100 and had them crucified. It is not surprising that Hamilcar was keen to protect himself from that possibility if the Roman terms proved unacceptably harsh.[32]

The Peace of Lutatius was a treaty intended to replace all other treaties between the two combatants. Initially, the Romans demanded that the Carthaginians leave Sicily entirely and commit to never attacking Syracuse or Rome's allies.[33] In addition, Carthage was required to pay

[30] Polybius, *Histories,* I.58
[31] *Lazenby, 1996, p. 149*
[32] *Lazenby, 1996, p. 149*
[33] Polybius, I.62.8-9.

Rome 2,200 Euboean silver talents, approximately 56 tons, over a 20-year period as reparations. The Carthaginian troops were to lay down all weapons, and any Roman deserters were to be handed over. Hamilcar refused the last two conditions. Lutatius then threatened to have the Carthaginian troops pass under the yoke.[34] Hamilcar still would not agree. Lutatius relented, and Carthaginian soldiers were later allowed to leave Sicily under arms.[35] In effect, Hamilcar secured the concession that the Carthaginian Army could retire without tokens of submission.[36]

The Comitia Centuriata in Rome, however, would not ratify the agreement negotiated, and a commission led by Quantius Lutatius Cerco, brother of the consul and consul himself in 240 BCE, amended the treaty and added new conditions.[37] Carthage would evacuate all islands between Italy and Sicily and pay 2,200 silver talents in ten-year installments, with 1,000 talents to be paid upfront. Carthaginians held by Rome were to be ransomed, but any Romans held by Carthage had to be freed without payment.[38] All Carthaginian warships were excluded from Italian coastal waters and those of their allies. The injunction not to make war on allies was retained in the new proposals, and a directive banning Carthaginian involvement in the internal affairs of allies was added.

There were further detailed conditions, including a provision that neither side would seek to recruit soldiers, levy tributes, or build public buildings on the other's territories.[39] Polybius suggests this final clause replaced the one specifying that Carthage would not attack Syracuse. Hamilcar argued for the clause, possibly to save face, given that the new conditions imposed by Rome were harsher than those originally agreed upon. Alongside his forces in Drepana and Eryx at Lilybaeum, Hamilcar surrendered, and he returned to Carthage, leaving Gisco to organize the evacuation of mercenaries to Africa. When he reached Carthage, he announced his retirement. However, his mercenaries were unhappy at what they considered to be his abandoning them, and they were not prepared to simply accept the situation.

The Mercenary War

The result of the First Punic War was a complete dearth of cash in Carthage, which was a serious problem because Carthage relied chiefly on mercenary armies. Thousands of mercenaries throughout the Carthaginian Empire were suddenly not getting their wages, and the result was inevitable: war. An all-out insurrection of mercenary contingents throughout the Punic Empire, including Iberia, Sardinia and Corsica, and a renewed attack from the subjugated Lybian tribes followed. Suddenly, Carthage was fighting for her very life and grudgingly accepting military and financial aid from her two old enemies, Syracuse and Rome.

---

[34] Diodorus Siculus, XXIV.13; Cornelius Nepos, *Hamilcar*, I.5.
[35] Polybius, I.20.6-1442.
[36] Polybius, I.62.8.
[37] Valerius Maximus, I.3.
[38] Eutropius, II.27.4.
[39] Polybius, III.27.2-3.

Ironically, Hamilcar's success had made the Mercenary War possible in the first place. Hamilcar was not defeated in Sicily in the conventional sense, so the number of his troops had not been reduced to any great extent, leaving an army of approximately 20,000 angry and frustrated soldiers wanting the pay due them. Hamilcar organized the return of troops to Carthage through General Hasdrubal Gisco, arranging for practical, small groups to be sent at a time. Hamilcar's thinking was that the city would spread out the payments, avoiding direct clashes and preventing the whole force from joining together.[40] Carthaginian authorities, however, waited until the whole army had gathered, probably in the summer of 241 BCE, and tried to get the mercenaries to accept less than Hamilcar had promised.

As the strain of maintaining the army increased, Carthaginian authorities sent the mercenaries off to Sicca, once more pleading with them to forgo all of their unpaid wages because the settlement with Rome had impoverished the city.[41] The discipline Hamilcar achieved with the mercenaries had broken down, and when Hanno II the Great made it absolutely clear that Carthage would not honor Hamilcar's promises over wages, they marched on Tunis in September 241 BCE The mercenaries also refused to accept Hamilcar as an arbitrator, angered by his refusal to accompany his army from Sicily and his retirement to Carthage as soon as the treaty with Rome had been formalized.[42]

Panicking at the nearness of such a hostile force, the Senate agreed to pay in full, but the mercenaries responded by demanding even more. Gisco, who had a good reputation with the army, was brought over from Sicily in late 241 BCE and sent to the camp with enough money to pay most of what was owed. He distributed what he had available and promised that the balance would be paid as soon as possible. It is highly probable the revolt would have ended at that point if not for Spendius and Mathos's intervention.

Spendius was an escaped Roman slave who had joined the Carthaginian Army in the First Punic War at some point prior to 241 BCE Spendius's date of birth is unknown, as are most details of his activities prior to his coming to prominence as the mutiny's leader, but he was elected co-general with the African Mathos. Mathos was a Libyan, recruited into the Carthaginian Army during the First Punic War like Spendius, at some point prior to 241 BCE[43] As an African, he was well-placed to incite rebellion between Carthage's North African possessions, and they responded to his call by providing him with provisions, money, and 70,000 troops.

The ensuing war lasted four years. Hamilcar was appointed joint commander of the Carthaginian Army alongside Hanno, but there was no cooperation between the two.[44] While

---

[40] Polybius, I.66.2-4.
[41] Polybius, I.66.550.
[42] Goldsworthy, 2006, pp. 121-122
[43] Hoyos, 2007

Hanno confronted Mathos in the north near Hippo, Hamilcar concentrated on retaking towns defecting to the rebels. Spendius continued to avoid any large battles, which proved wise as when he was eventually brought to a battle, he lost over 10,000 men, and 4,000 were captured.[45] From the time of his appointment, Hamilcar offered captured mercenaries the option of joining his army or being transported to their homelands. The two rebel leaders decided that such leniency could well undermine their forces, so to prompt a reaction from Hamilcar, they had 700 Carthaginian prisoners, including Gisco, tortured to death. They had their hands cut off, they were castrated, their legs were broken, and they were thrown into a pit and buried alive.[46]

As intended, the Carthaginians killed their prisoners, and from then on, neither side showed any mercy. The unusual ferocity of the fighting caused Polybius to term it the "Truceless War."[47] Any further prisoners taken by the Carthaginians were trampled to death by elephants.[48]

The Carthaginians eventually trapped Spendius in a pass known as the Saw. Without any supplies or the possibility of getting any, the rebels ate their horses, their prisoners, and then their slaves, hoping Mathos would rescue them from his base in Tunis. Spendius and Autaritus finally arranged a meeting with Hamilcar to discuss terms of surrender. The whole entourage was taken prisoner and crucified within sight of the defenders in Tunis. The leaderless rebels then attempted to fight their way out in the Battle of the Saw and were massacred.

In 239 BCE, the previously loyal cities of Utica and Hippo murdered their Carthaginian garrisons and joined the rebels. The Romans declined the city's offer to occupy it. It was at that point that Mathos made the decision to move his base of operations to Tunis.[49] Hamilcar laid siege to Tunis in late 238 BCE, but he abandoned it soon thereafter. Despite the siege being lifted, few supplies were getting through, and Mathos decided the situation untenable. He led the army to the port city of Leptis Parva, just south of the modern city of Monastir in Tunisia. Hanno and Hamilcar finally agreed to work together, and their combined forces marched after them with an army of 25,000, including every Carthaginian citizen of military age.[50] Mathos decided to gamble everything on one battle, but it was a disastrous loss. Hamilcar and Hanno agreed that, on this occasion, they would not execute those captured. Instead, they would be sold into slavery. Mathos was, however, different. After his capture, he was dragged through the streets of Carthage before being tortured to death.[51]

---

[44] *Miles, 2010*

[45] Bagnall, 1999
[46] Eckstein, 2017
[47] Polybius, I.66.
[48] *Miles, 2010, p. 210*
[49] Goldsworthy, 2006
[50] Bagnall, 1999
[51] Hoyos, 2007

A modern depiction of Spendius being crucified

Iberia

As the Mercenary War was coming to a close, Carthage was hit by a series of other disasters in 239 BCE. Its fleet and supply flotilla bringing supplies from Emporia sunk in a storm, and more significantly, the mercenaries in Sardinia rebelled. The rebels besieged Boaster, and when it fell, all Carthaginians defending the citadel were executed. All Carthaginian territories in Sardinia were captured, one by one. Carthage sent a newly-recruited mercenary force under Hanno to retake the island in 239 BCE, but they, too, rebelled, killing Hanno and the Carthaginian officers. The rebels then asked Rome to take over Sardinia, but they were refused, as was a similar request from Utica.

Up to that point, Rome had scrupulously adhered to the terms of the treaty that ended the First Punic War and even sent supplies to Carthage to help with the fight during the Mercenary War. The mercenaries in Sardinia did not treat the local population well, thus provoking them to turn on the rebels, and they were successful in forcing them to leave the island in 237 BCE when they retreated to mainland Italy and again asked Rome to support them in retaking the island. On that occasion, despite treaty obligations, the Romans seized Sardinia and Corsica and demanded that Carthage pay 1,200 talents for its refusal to renounce its claim on the islands. The local population on both islands tried to fight off the Roman takeover, but without assistance from Carthage, it was an impossible task. The Romans' actions set the scene for the Second Punic War, but the more immediate consequences were felt in Carthage itself.[52]

The aristocratic party had dominated Carthaginian politics since 248 BCE, with its nobles consistently advocating a policy of appeasement with Rome, even if it meant giving up territories. The policy was to minimize Sicilian operations while Hamilcar was in command, reduce the navy, and support Hanno II's conquests in Africa. This approach contributed to Carthage's ultimate defeat in the First Punic War. They had remained in power throughout the Mercenary War and generally opposed Hamilcar's more aggressive policies. Hamilcar did, however, have his supporters, particularly in the mercantile class, whose interests lay in holding onto Carthaginian-controlled territory. Hamilcar's son-in-law, Hasdrubal the Fair, emerged as the nominal leader of the group, but it was Hamilcar who shaped policy.

Flying in the face of facts, the aristocratic party blamed the loss in the First Punic War, the mismanagement of the mercenaries that had led to the Mercenary War, and the rebellion in Sardinia on Hamilcar, but the popularity he enjoyed amongst the people thwarted any attempt to put him on trial. Hamilcar, along with Hasdrubal, managed to engineer a restriction of the power of the aristocracy and secure immunity from prosecution for himself and his officers.

Hamilcar's faction was strong enough to ensure that he could implement his next plans. While he prioritized the payment of the war indemnity so the Romans would have no excuse to interfere in Carthaginian affairs, he firmly believed that further conflict with Rome was inevitable, and he began preparing Carthage for that eventuality. He obtained permission from the Senate to recruit and train a new army, ostensibly to secure Carthage's North African possessions, when he, in fact, had a far more ambitious goal in mind.

Hamilcar decided that the way to restore Carthage's power and prepare for the next round with Rome was to develop its Spanish assets and become a more overt imperial power. Spain was rich in timber, mines, and men, and he believed that the Romans could hardly object if they wanted Carthage to continue paying the huge war reparations demanded of Carthage if it tried to

---

[52] Bagnall, 1999

increase its revenues. Just as importantly, Hamilcar recognized that even if the Carthaginians lacked the necessary sea power, Italy could be reached directly by land from Spain, which might prove invaluable in future conflicts.

The fact that Spain was some distance from both Carthage and Rome also appealed to Hamilcar, who intended to build surreptitiously for the future. Without the consent of the Carthaginian Senate, he ferried his army from North Africa to Gades in 236 BCE, where he hoped to build a new empire to compensate Carthage for the loss of Sicily and Sardinia. Prior to his departure from Carthage, Hamilcar made sacrifices to the gods.[53]

Though he was a child, Hannibal had begged his father to accompany the expedition to Spain. At first, it appears as though Hamilcar was reluctant to let someone so young join him on his campaign, but due to repeated pleas by Hannibal, he seems to have relented. Whatever his reasons, the young Hannibal was certainly with the Carthaginian army when it marched along the coast of North Africa to the strait of Gibraltar, where, under Hamilcar's supervision, the troops were ferried across the narrow strait and onto Spanish soil. The journey took Hamilcar's army some months, but at the time the Carthaginian navy was in such a parlous state that there were simply not enough ships available to transport the army by sea from Carthage itself, leading Hamilcar to take the longer coastal route.

Hamilcar landed at Gades in the summer of 237 BCE at a time when Carthage had lost control of the territories it had before the First Punic War, so Hamilcar presented the military invasion as simply retaking what Carthage had previously held.[54] Phoenician settlements - founded, in many cases centuries earlier along the Atlantic and Mediterranean coasts of southern Spain - were, in the main, trading posts. Although they might control a limited area around the settlement, they had no direct control over the tribes inhabiting the wider areas of the peninsula.[55]

At this time, many of the Iberian and Celtiberian tribes were not unified and notoriously warlike. In addition, the Phoenicians had been in competition with the Greeks - especially those from Massalia - in trade and the foundation of settlements.[56] Phocaean Greeks had built colonies in Catalonia, at Mainke near Málaga, and three colonies near the mouth of Sucro. The rivalry between the Greeks and Phoenicians had led to the Phoenicians allying with the Etruscans to push the Greeks out of Corsica and destroy the colony at Mainke. By 490 BCE, Massalia had defeated Carthage twice, and a boundary along Cape Nao in Iberia was agreed upon.[57] Massalia became closer to Rome over the years, and by 237 BCE, the two were allies in all but name. This relationship was a significant factor in the politics of the region.

---

[53] Polybius III.11; Livy XXI.1.4.
[54] Strabo, *Geography*, V.158.
[55] Lancel, 1997
[56] Thucydides, *History of the Peloponnesian War*, I.13.6.
[57] Justin, XLIII.5.

Hamilcar's immediate objective in Iberia was to gain access to the gold and silver mines of the Sierra Morena.[58] Negotiations with the Tartessian tribes proved successful, probably because they had well-established links with the Phoenicians and their heirs, the Carthaginians. Tartessos - or Tartessus - at the mouth of the Guadalquivir River was a harbor city controlling the Iberian Peninsula's south coast. This is mentioned in sources from Greece and the Near East beginning in the first millennium BCE[59] Archaeological finds in the region have confirmed that the Tartesian culture was well-established, and to date, 97 inscriptions have been discovered in the Tartessian language. The Tartessians were also rich in metal, and in the 4th century BCE, the historian Ephorus describes Tartessos as having a plentiful supply of tin, gold, and copper brought from Celtic lands.[60] Trade in tin was vital since it is an essential component of bronze and is comparatively rare.

Several early sources refer to Tartessos as a river. Herodotus claimed that it rose in the Pyrenees and flowed out to sea outside the Pillars of Hercules.[61] However, no such river now flows, and there is no evidence that one ever did. Writing in the 2nd century CE, Pausanias gave specific details of the location of the city: "They say that Tartessus [sic] is a river in the land of the Iberians, running down into the sea by two mouths and that between these two mouths lies a city of the same name. The river, which is the largest in Iberia and tidal, those of a later day called Baetis and there are some who think that Tartessus was the ancient name of Carpia, a city of the Iberians."[62]

The river, known in his day as the Baetis, is now the Guadalquivir. One theory is that Tartessos may have been buried under the shifting wetlands. The river delta has been gradually blocked by a sandbar stretching from the mouth of the Rio Tinto near Palos de la Frontera to the riverbank opposite Sanlúcar de Barrameda. In the 1st century CE, Pliny the Elder incorrectly identified the city of Carteia as Tartessos.[63]

Gades was deliberately built by the Phoenicians to be near Tartessos on the island of Erytheia, northwest of Gibraltar at the tip of the Iberian Peninsula. It is thought to be one of the most ancient of cities still standing in Western Europe. Some sources place its founding by the Phoenicians of Tyre in the 8th century BCE, while others suggest it might date from around 1100 BCE. It was primarily a seasonal trading post, providing the Phoenicians with access to the vast mineral wealth of the area.

Perhaps unsurprisingly, the Greeks and Romans did not accept the Phoenician version of the city's origins, claiming it had been founded as a result of one of the 12 Labors of Hercules, the

---

[58] Lancel, 1997
[59] Herodotus, *The Histories,* I.163; IV.152.
[60] Freeman, 2010
[61] Herodotus, *The History*, i. 163 ; iv.152.
[62] Pausanias, *Description of Greece*, VI. 19.3.
[63] Pliny the Elder, *Natural History*, III.7.

10th of which required him to capture the cattle owned by the three-headed monster Geryon and take them to Eurystheus, the king of Mycenae.[64] This labor involved his traveling the known world, and when he arrived at the western end of the Mediterranean, he created the Pillars of Hercules, also known as the Gates of Cadiz or Gades. After capturing the cattle, Hercules built a huge mountain, and when he split it apart, he brought about the separation of the continents of Europe and Africa, thereby connecting the Mediterranean Sea to the Atlantic Ocean via the Strait of Gibraltar. The legend does not actually address the issue of who built the city, but all archaeological evidence indicates it was the Phoenicians.

The city became a battleground for control of the western Mediterranean Sea. With the decline of the Phoenicians in the east and the rise of Carthage in the west, the status of Gades changed, and in 500 BCE, it was integrated into the growing Carthaginian Empire. This provided Hamilcar with a ready-made base for his forays into southern Iberia. However, his negotiations were not as successful with the Turduli/Turdetani as they had been with Tartessos. Quoted by Strabo in the 1st century CE, Pytheas claimed the ancestral homeland of the Turduli was located north of Turdetania, the region where the kingdom of Tartessos was located in the Baetis River valley.[65] The Turdetani - or Turduli - tribe near the foothills of modern Seville and Córdoba were implacably opposed to Hamilcar. They had support from a number of Celtiberian tribes and were under the command of Istolacio. Hamilcar defeated these allied tribes, killed the leaders, and either released captured prisoners or incorporated them into his own army.[66]

His next opponent was another confederation of Celtic tribes, but this time, their leader was Indortes, possibly Istolacio's brother, who was able to field a force of nearly 50,000. Immediately after defeating the Turduli, Hamilcar invaded the land of the Lusitanians and the Vetones, part of modern-day Portugal, without opposition, but when he returned to the south, Indortes was waiting with his army. Despite his numerical advantage, Indortes retreated to higher ground. The Carthaginians surrounded him, and battle commenced. Indortes, and much of his army, turned tail and escaped. Hamilcar pursued and captured Indortes, had him tortured, blinded, and finally, crucified.[67] Hamilcar continued with this policy of inflicting savage cruelty on leaders opposing him but offering generous terms to the ordinary troops. After defeating Indortes, 10,000 erstwhile foes joined Hamilcar, and all local cities allied with him.

Having secured control over the mines as well as the river routes of Guadalquiver and Guadalete, giving access to the mining area, Gades began minting silver coins in 237 BCE, but Carthaginians took control of the mines and introduced new technologies to increase the production.[68] Control of the mines meant that Hamilcar could pay for his mercenary army, as

---

[64] Diodorus Siculus, IV.11.1; Appollodorus, *Library,* II.4.11.
[65] Strabo, *Geography*, III.2.11.
[66] Diodorus Siculus, XXV.10.1.
[67] Diodorus Siculus, XXV.10.2.

[68] *Miles, 2010*

well as send silver ore back to Carthage to help pay off the war indemnity. In so doing, he stifled any excuse Rome might have had for interference in Carthaginian affairs. Hamilcar quickly consolidated his position in southern Iberia to the extent that, in 236 BCE, he could send Hasdrubal the Fair with an army to Africa to put down a Numidian rebellion. Hasdrubal defeated the rebels, killing 8,000 and taking 2,000 prisoners, before returning to Iberia.

After subduing Turdetania, Hamilcar moved east toward Cape Nao, meeting fierce resistance all along his route. Even previously friendly tribes, such as the Bastetani, refused to allow him unchallenged progress through their land. There followed four years of constant campaigning, resulting in the total subjugation of the area between Gades and Cape Nao. During those years, Hamilcar created a professional army of Iberians, Africans, Numidians, and other mercenaries that his son, Hannibal, would later lead across the Alps. By 231 BCE, Hamilcar had consolidated his Iberian territorial gains and founded the city of Akra Leuke, modern-day Alicante.[69] In securing the area, Hamilcar also took over areas surrounding a number of Massalian colonies near the mouth of Sucro River.[70] Massalia was so alarmed by the Carthaginian advance that it reported its concerns to the Romans, who finally decided to investigate the matter.

While Hamilcar was busy campaigning in Iberia, Rome was busy trying to consolidate its control in Sardinia, Corsica, and Liguria, where the locals continued to put up stiff resistance to the Roman occupation. Rome suspected the Carthaginians of aiding the insurrectionists and sent embassies to Carthage in 236, 235, 233, and 230 BCE, accusing them of interference and threatening reprisals if it did not stop. In 231 BCE, a Roman embassy was sent to Hamilcar in Spain to inquire about what he was up to and what his intentions in the peninsula were. Hamilcar replied that his only goal was to gather enough booty to pay off the war indemnity.[71] The Romans were apparently happy with his assurances and withdrew.

Hamilcar's campaigns continued successfully, and he even began to consolidate his gains by founding a string of cities, including, popular legend has it, the port city of Barcino (from Barca, his family name), on the site of modern-day Barcelona. After the foundation of Akra Leuke, Hamilcar moved northwest, but there are no records of his subsequent campaigns.

During this time, Hannibal grew to adolescence, tutored in warfare by Greek instructors who instructed him by detailing the conquests of Alexander the Great, Alcibiades, and Pyrrhus of Epirus, all of whom he would come to greatly admire and hold in high esteem. Of course, Hannibal also witnessed his father Hamilcar's successes as a commander firsthand. It is likely that Hamilcar himself, when campaign matters permitted, would have taken time to instruct his son himself, for they appear to have been close. Indeed, Hamilcar was determined that Hannibal himself, when the time came, should take up his mantle and proceed with the crusade that had

---

[69] Astin, 1989, p. 23
[70] Livy, XXIV.14.3–4.
[71] Cassius Dio, fr4813.

occupied most of his military life: the destruction of Rome. Hamilcar had never recovered from the humiliation of being defeated by the Republic's forces, and he longed for the day when he might lead Carthage's troops against Rome once again. To this end, he spent much time instilling in his son an implacable hatred of Carthage's sworn enemy. Such was Hamilcar's zeal for his cause, and his desire to bind his son to it, that he had Hannibal accompany him to a shrine in the town of Peniscola (near modern Valencia) and bid him swear upon the altar that he would be Rome's enemy forever. Hannibal duly did so, adding, "As soon as I have come of age, I swear that I will bring Rome low by fire and the sword."

In the winter of 228 BCE, Hasdrubal the Fair was sent on a separate campaign while Hamilcar besieged an Iberian town before sending most of his troops to winter quarters at Akra Leuke. Meanwhile, the leadership of Celtic tribes opposed to Hamilcar fell to Orissus. The first mention of him is in reference to the aid he provided to the city of Heliké, which was besieged by Hamilcar in 228 BCE.[72] He may have fought alongside Istolacio and Indortes, but he was an able and cunning commander, more so than either of them. Orissus pretended to want an alliance with Hamilcar, but as soon as he felt the Carthaginians had lowered their guard, he attacked and dealt Hamilcar his first defeat in Iberia. The Carthaginians tried to use their war elephants in battle, but Orissus came up with a strategy to counter them by driving a herd of fighting bulls with torches on their horns into the elephants. The elephants stampeded in panic, causing chaos in the Carthaginian lines and burning their camp.

For some historians, this is the battle in which Hamilcar died, but there are other accounts. For example, those by Diodorus and Appian say he drowned in a river when he fell from his horse while being pursued by the Oretans.[73] Zonaras asserted that Hamilcar died in the Carthaginian camp while escaping from his own rampaging elephants.[74] Finally, Polybius argued that all of these accounts are false and Hamilcar survived the battle but was killed sometime later in another battle against Iberian tribesmen.[75]

Modern historians believe it is likely Hamilcar died in battle against the Vettoni, who lived across the Tagus, west of Toledo, north of Turduli, and northwest of Oretani territory.[76] His death would be avenged the following year in 227 BCE, when Orissus was decisively beaten by Hasdrubal the Fair, commanding an army of 50,000 men, 6,000 horsemen, and 200 elephants. Orissus was executed on the basis that he had been the primary cause of Hamilcar's death, and the 12 cities he controlled had fallen to the Carthaginians.[77]

---

[72] *Indortes e Istolacio, Orisón, Indíbil y Mandonio* by AA Pérez (1988).
[73] Diodorus, XXV.10.3-4; Appian, *Iberia*, VI.1.5.
[74] Zonaras, VIII.18.
[75] Polybius, II.1.8.
[76] Cornelius Nepos, *Hamilcar*, IV.2.
[77] Diodorus Siculus, XXV.12.

Hamilcar's Lasting Legacy

In a relatively short span of eight years, Hamilcar had secured a large expanse of territory in Iberia using a combination of military force and diplomacy, and despite his premature death, he succeeded in restoring Carthage's financial situation to the extent that it could contemplate fighting Rome again. As such, Hamilcar's plan to extend Carthaginian control over more of Iberia did not, end upon his death.

Hamilcar's son-in-law, Hasdrubal, took command in the wake of Hamilcar's death and quickly took territory up to the River Ebro. The Greek colonies became even more agitated, and they appealed to Massalia, who then appealed to Rome to curtail the Carthaginian aggression.

At the time, Rome had no territory in either Gaul or Spain, which meant their concerns were primarily economic and related to the possibility that Carthage could regain the pre-eminent position it had held prior to the First Punic War. A very specific problem was tin, which was a highly strategic material because a mixture of 10% tin to 90% copper was needed to make bronze, the essential alloy used to make non-rusting weapons. Copper was readily available but tin, for Massalia, came almost exclusively from Cornwall. The route from Cornwall was via Brittany and then down the west coast of Gaul, skirting the Pyrenees, then around Carcassonne before reaching its destination. Both the Massalians and the Romans were concerned that any Carthaginian advance beyond the Ebro would put this vital trade route at considerable risk.

In 226 BCE, a Roman delegation met with Hasdrubal to negotiate a settlement of the issue. At that meeting, it was agreed that the Roman sphere of influence would extend as far as the northern bank of the Ebro, while Carthaginian influence was to stop at the southern bank. However, there was one problem, in the form of Zakynthos (later Saguntum). This Greek city lay south of the Ebro, putting it within the Carthaginian sphere of influence, but it would prove pivotal in leading the Carthaginians and Romans to renew their hostilities in what became the Second Punic War.

It appears likely that around 225 BCE, Hasdrubal began plotting with the Gauls of the Po Valley in the north of Italy (the only as yet unconquered area in the Italian Peninsula) to launch an attack on Rome with Carthaginian backing, but the Senate got wind of the plan and ordered a preemptive strike of their own, leading to a five-year war which eventually led to the annexation of the Po Valley. Hasdrubal himself was assassinated in 221, possibly with Roman collusion.

Rather than solve the Romans' problems, however, Hasdrubal's death brought about the rise of the most famous Carthaginian of all. Hasdrubal was succeeded by his brother-in-law and Hamilcar's son, Hannibal. In the history of war, only a select few men always make the list of greatest generals, and one of them is Hannibal, who holds the distinction of being the only man to nearly bring Rome to its knees before its collapse almost 700 years later.

In 237 BCE, legend has it that when Hamilcar was about to set off to Spain, Hannibal, then nine years old, begged his father to take him with him. Hamilcar was about to offer a sacrifice to the gods to ensure the success of his campaign, and although he refused his son's request, he did place Hannibal's hand on the animal to be sacrificed and asked him to swear that he would never forget that Rome was the enemy.[78]

Whether that legend is true, the Barcids no doubt felt Carthaginian humiliation at the hands of the Romans very deeply, and all of Hamilcar's sons opposed Rome throughout their lives.[79] Hannibal proved to be a natural military genius and a leader who inspired his men with his personal bravery and his willingness to share all their daily hardships. He was elected as leader by the troops without the permission of the Carthaginian Senate, but the politicians at home could not do anything other than endorse their choice. This method of choosing their own leader reinforces the idea that leadership in the Iberian Peninsula was a kind of personal dictatorship vested in the Barca family.

Cornelius Nepos claimed that Hannibal was a scholar as well as a soldier, and this assertion ties in with the level of statesmanship that he exhibited in the latter part of his career. [80] He was taught Greek by Sosilos and it is said he wrote books in Greek.

[78] Livy, *The History of Rome*, XXI
[79] Livy, *The History of Rome*, XXI, I.
[80] Cornelius Nepos, *Lives of the Eminent Commanders: Hannibal.*

A bust believed to depict Hannibal

For two years, Hannibal bided his time, consolidating his position in the Iberian Peninsula and massing his forces, abiding by one of the greatest military truths and one which doubtless his tutors and his father, with their tales of Alexander and Alcibiades, had contributed to instill in him: numbers do not matter so much as concentration of force. After all, the army sizes don't matter if troops are not available to fight in one single critical location at any given time.

Meanwhile, even as Hannibal was preparing to strike out against their very heart, the Romans seem to have grown unusually complacent. To a sense this may have been rational, as Hannibal was new to overall command, and with both Hamilcar and Hasdrubal dead, the Romans must have felt themselves secure.

The troops that Hannibal commanded were professional soldiers who fought for pay and plunder rather than any particular state or political ideal. They comprised a relatively small number of Carthaginians, Gauls, Africans and Iberians. The typical Greek phalanx was the core of the army and its tactics derived from the hoplite warfare practiced in Greece. However, the most distinctive troops were the Balearic slingers. They used pebbles or leaden bullets and were accurate both over short and long range. It is said that they could hit a target at distances that archers could not match. Their overall firepower was well in excess of anything that contemporary archers could match.

The Spaniards tended to provide heavy cavalry with two men on horseback, one to fight from the horse and the other to dismount and fight on foot. The Numidians, who came mainly from Algeria and Morocco, were considered the most fearsome of the Carthaginian troops. The term Numidian stems from the word nomad and they were expert horsemen. Their light cavalry units were swift and they developed a tactic of charge and retreat, charge and retreat that heavily armed hoplite troops could not counter.

The most famous Carthaginian units were the fighting elephants. Unlike most fighting elephants previously used in war, which were Indian, the Carthaginian ones were African of the cyclotis variety known as forest elephants to distinguish them from the larger bush elephants found in central and southern Africa. They were first used by the Carthaginians in the First Punic War at Agrigentum in Sicily in 262 BCE and thereafter were a feature of all Carthaginian armies.[81]

When Hannibal first took command of the Carthaginian forces, there was still considerable consolidation work to be done in Spain before he could turn his attention to Rome. In 221 BCE he besieged the Oclades capital of Carteia. The Oclades tribal area was located south of the Ebro, so in the Carthaginian sphere of influence, but it had not yet been absorbed into the territory controlled by them. By taking this area, he moved right up to the agreed border of Carthaginian-Roman spheres of influence. More importantly for later relationships with Rome, this annexation meant that the city of Saguntum was now surrounded by Carthaginian territory. At the time of the agreement between Rome and Carthage that designated their respective areas, Saguntum, while south of the Ebro, was not adjacent to any Carthaginian territory. Part of the Ebro Treaty stated that "neither side should extend its dominion beyond the Ebro while Saguntum, situated between the empires of the two peoples, should be preserved in independence."[82] Saguntum, along with other Greek cities in the northern part of the east coast that were also concerned about Carthaginian ambitions, allied themselves with Rome for protection.

---

[81] P. 57, *The First Punic War: a military history* by J. F. Lazenby (1996). Stanford University Press.
[82] Livy, *History of Rome*, 21.2.7.

For the time being, however, Hannibal left Saguntum to its own devices and turned his attention to the north of Spain. He crossed the Sierra Morena, past Merida to Salamantica, modern Salamanca, which he captured. He defeated the Vaccaei, a tribe based around the River Doro, and then turned south again towards Toledo.[83] The Iberians combined to attack him as he crossed the Tagus, but Hannibal slipped past them and came up behind their lines. The Iberians were routed, and this victory brought the whole of Iberia south of the Ebro under Carthaginian control with the notable exception of Saguntum.[84]

Having secured his base, Hannibal turned his thoughts to how he might implement the plan Hamilcar had conceived to defeat Rome. It combined the elements of initiative and surprise with shock. The main feature of this audacious plan was none other than the concept that the next war with the Romans had to be fought on Italian soil, and the route to Italy had never looked as possible as it did in the first years of Hannibal's leadership. The Gauls, in northern Italy, were already in a state of ferment, and as recently as 225 BCE, an alliance of Gallic tribes had invaded Etruria, defeating a Roman army at Faesolae and going on to ravage the countryside. To prevent further invasions, the Senate had ordered the invasion of Cisalpine Gaul, but the Romans insisted on unconditional surrender and, in due course, Cisalpine Gaul became a province.

Roman colonies were established in the newly acquired territory at Placentia, now Piacenza, Cremona, and Mutina, now Modena, to act as a check on the Gauls. Hannibal knew that the Gauls felt humiliated by their defeats and the foundation of Roman colonies, and he was determined to profit from this unrest. He was also aware that the Romans had further difficulties in Illyria and Greece. It seems that the Romans never entertained the thought that the Carthaginians might launch an overland attack on Italy, an attack that would mean crossing the Ebro, the Pyrenees, Gaul, the Rhone, and the Alps to reach their target. Of course, that is precisely what Hannibal was determined to do.

Hannibal planned his operation in great secrecy, and the details were worked out meticulously. He gathered information on his intended route to Italy and assessed the fighting capabilities of all potential foes he might encounter on his march.[85] As well as gathering military intelligence, he gathered political intelligence about all the tribes he might have to deal with. He was, naturally, particularly keen to learn of any aversion to Roman rule. All of this information was crucial if he was to plan for a successful march to a destination over 1,000 miles from his base. Practical issues such as how his army was to be fed until it reached what he assumed would be the welcoming arms of the Cisalpine Gauls were thought through in minute detail. It is rumored that one of his commanders, Hannibal Monomachus, suggested that the troops should be trained in how to live off human flesh, which, if true, was quickly dismissed by Hannibal.[86]

---

[83] Polybius, *Histories*, III.14.5-8.
[84] Livy, *History of Rome*, 21.5.6-16.
[85] Livy, *History of Rome*, 21.5.
[86] Polybius, *Histories*, IX.

Although Hannibal could rely on the loyalty of his troops, he faced difficulty in persuading the Carthaginian Senate to support his plans. The Senate had numerous members who were determined to maintain the peace with Rome at any price and a number who resented the Barca family's domination of Iberia. Hannibal was reasonably certain that the Senate would never declare war on Rome, and he knew he had to manipulate the situation to achieve his goal.

Hannibal supported an Iberian tribe that had a dispute with Saguntum, and the Saguntines immediately appealed to Rome for help under the terms of the Ebro Treaty, fearing a Carthaginian attack. The Roman Senate duly sent a delegation to Hannibal to remind him that Saguntum was under Roman protection.[87] By the time the envoys arrived in Spain in 219 BCE, Hannibal had already laid siege to the city and claimed to be too busy to meet with them. His hope was that the Romans would declare war there and then, but instead the envoys withdrew and sailed to Carthage to complain about their treatment, demand a cessation of hostilities against Saguntum, and ask for Hannibal to be handed over to atone for the breach of the treaty that had ended the First Punic War.[88] Hannibal had alerted his supporters in the Carthaginian Senate of the impending arrival of the Roman delegation, and, forewarned, they ensured that when Rome's demands were made known to the whole Senate, they took immediate offense and declared that the Saguntines were the ones at fault and that it would be most unwise of Rome to side with them and render null and void the good relations that had been built up in the years following the end of the war.

While all of this diplomacy was going on, Hannibal continued with the siege and duly breached its defenses after eight months. The city was treated savagely, with the population massacred and their belongings looted. Hannibal sent the captured booty back to Carthage to bolster support for his actions.[89] The Roman envoys returned to Rome with Carthage's answer to their demands at approximately the same time news reached Rome of the fall and subsequent sacking of Saguntum. The Roman Senate was incensed and voted to declare war on Carthage, but before engaging in direct conflict, it sent new envoys to Carthage to ascertain whether Hannibal's actions at Saguntum had been carried out on his own initiative or whether they had the support of the Senate.[90]

The Carthaginians replied with a legal argument claiming that the treaty between Carthage and Rome required both parties to refrain from interfering with the allies of the other and that the treaty made no specific mention of Saguntum being an ally of Rome. They also argued that the treaty had never actually been ratified by the Roman Senate. The senior Roman envoy was Quintus Fabius Maximus, who, clearly frustrated by what he regarded as Carthaginian obfuscation, said, "Here we bring you peace or war. Choose which you prefer."[91] The

---

[87] Polybius, *Histories*, III.15.5.
[88] Livy, *History of Rome*, 21.6.
[89] Livy, *History of Rome*, 21.10-15.
[90] Polybius, *Histories*, III.21.6.
[91] Livy, *History of Rome,* 21.

Carthaginians replied that the Romans could choose. Fabius said, "War." The Carthaginians responded, "So be it."[92] Through Hannibal's machinations, the Romans declared the Second Punic War, and on that basis it could be claimed that it was the Romans who had violated the peace treaty.

Either way, in the spring of 218 BCE, at the head of approximately 50,000 infantry, 15,000 cavalry, and 50 war elephants, Hannibal began marching northeast. His plan was breathtakingly ambitious: he would march through the Pyrenees, across southern Gaul, over the Alps and into Italy proper, thereby avoiding the heavily fortified border in the northwest of Italy. It was a route no general had ever taken before, let alone a general with so many animals (including elephants). His father Hamilcar had been defeated trying to invade southern Italy and attempting to outfight the Roman navy at sea, but Hannibal would not make the same mistake.

Pushing aside with contemptuous ease the stiff resistance of the Pyrenean tribes, who contested every step of the way from their strongholds of the mountain passes, Hannibal pushed forwards with remarkable speed, leaving behind a detachment of some 10,000 Iberian soldiers to keep his lines of communication open and pacify the tumultuous region. He then marched on into southern Gaul, negotiating with the local chieftains and outfighting those who had a mind to contest his advance. His speed of maneuver and his ability to move his army across rough terrain proved unmatched in the ancient world since the time of Alexander the Great. By that point, his army, which now numbered some 40,000 infantry, 8,000 cavalry, and around 40 war elephants, danced up the valley of the Rhone to evade a Roman force sent to bar his passage southwards through the strategically vital gap in the mountains where the Alps meet the Mediterranean. One of the most famous military campaigns in history was truly underway.

While it cannot be argued that Hannibal eclipsed Hamilcar, and Hamilcar is almost wholly remembered today simply for being Hannibal's father, it is only fair to note that Hamilcar was the most prominent military figure of his time and the best commander of the First Punic War. He was not just an able military strategist but an excellent diplomat and fervent patriot, and it seems he passed all of these qualities, along with his hatred of Rome, on to his son Hannibal, whom he specifically trained to carry the fight to Rome. Cato praised Hamilcar's abilities and ranked him above most leaders, including most Romans.[93] It was his personal influence among the mercenaries and surrounding African people, combined with his strategy, that enabled him to crush the revolt by 237 BCE amid a war marked by atrocities on both sides.

The terms upon which Rome insisted in the aftermath of the First Punic War and the support Rome provided in the Mercenary War might have ushered in a long period of peace between the two powers, but it was the seizure of Sardinia that ended this possibility, as far as Hamilcar was concerned. Polybius explicitly cites Hamilcar's attitude to the peace settlement as one of the

---

[92] Livy, *History of Rome*, 21.18.
[93] Plutarch, *Parallel Lives: Life of Cato the Elder*, VIII.14.

major factors in the outbreak of the Second Punic War. He documented Hamilcar's view that Carthage gave up on Sicily too soon and that Hamilcar remained undefeated and forced to make peace against his wishes.[94]

The subsequent Mercenary War, as far as Hamilcar was concerned, showed that Carthage had the military capacity to carry on a war. More importantly, it cemented his belief that - against Phoenician and Carthaginian tradition - if Carthage were to survive the Roman threat, it had to become a more overtly imperialist power. The military had to be expanded, and a standing army had to be created. For Hamilcar, the Roman occupation of Sardinia, followed by Corsica, simply proved that the Romans were duplicitous and could never be trusted, no matter what agreements or treaties they signed.[95] Hamilcar's success in Spain rebuilt Carthaginian finances and created the standing army he thought necessary, giving Carthage the means to take on Rome once again.

It might even be argued that Hamilcar's personal animosity would be Carthage's undoing. Without him, it is possible that the aristocratic party in Carthage would have reconciled itself to Roman supremacy and concentrated on securing and expanding the city's holdings in North Africa. Hamilcar was aggrieved by what he saw as the meek acceptance of Rome's dominance and the subsequent loss of islands that had been so important to Carthage for generations. It was his determination to rebuild Carthaginian strength that led to his unauthorized invasion of Iberia.

Hamilcar's influence on Hannibal obviously had a profound historical impact as well. Rome barely survived the Second Punic War, and Hamilcar's vision of a successful outcome in the war against Rome was nearly achieved. To survive, Rome had to adjust to meet the Carthaginian threat under Hannibal, and these changes helped pave the way for Rome to expand and conquer most of Europe. Thus, while some argue that Hamilcar's ultimate legacy was the destruction of his city, it is also possible that Rome would have ultimately adopted a policy of destroying Carthage anyway. If so, Hamilcar's strategies had at least given his city a chance of surviving the Punic Wars.

In concrete terms, Hamilcar's invasion of the Iberian Peninsula resulted in the foundation of a number of Spanish cities, including Cartagena, Alicante, and possibly Barcelona. At least two founding myths for Barcelona have been proposed by historians since the 15th century,[96] but the foundation of Cartagena is clear cut. By 227 BCE, it was founded as Qart Hadasht, meaning "New Town" in Carthaginian.

At the same time, Carthaginian intervention in the peninsula all but ensured the area would be subjected to Roman rule. Once the Carthaginian territories had been taken, those parts of Hispania became the two provinces of Hispania Citerior and Hispania Ulterior, which in turn were later subdivided into further provinces. They became some of the wealthiest and most

---

[94] Polybius, I.88.7.
[95] Polybius, III.10.4.
[96] Dietler & López-Ruiz, 2009, p. 75

Romanized of the empire's provinces, but the process by which the whole of Spain came under Roman rule was both violent and complex. Given that the Iberian Peninsula is Europe's second largest peninsula, maintaining control required vigorous efforts, including Roman-sponsored migrations by the Sueves, Alani, Vandals, Visigoths, and other tribes. For example, the Visigoths first set foot on the peninsula in 416 CE, where they were tasked with forcefully reinstituting Roman authority upon other Germanic invaders who had occupied the land. Initially, the Visigoths followed instructions to a tee, but as time progressed, it appeared that there may have been reason to have been suspicious of the Visigoths after all. In 418, they were relocated to France, where they established a makeshift kingdom of their own in Toulouse. When they inevitably noticed their employer's increasingly fragile authority, they realized it would not take much to squeeze the disintegrating empire out of the picture.

The ramifications of 600 years of Roman rule had significant consequences for the rest of the ancient world, and it had a profound impact on subsequent European history. In fact, it can be argued that those consequences are still being felt in Spain today when it comes to language, culture and political complications.

Inadvertently, that also helps ensure that the importance of one of Rome's most famous enemies also endures.

Online Resources

Other books about Rome by Charles River Editors

Other books about ancient history by Charles River Editors

Other books about the Punic Wars on Amazon

Further Reading

Antique Ships. (2017, October 12). Naval Encyclopedia. https://naval-encyclopedia.com/antique-ships.php

Astin, A.E. (1989). *The Cambridge Ancient History.* Cambridge University Press.

Aubet, M.E. (1987). *The Phoenicians and the West: Politics, Colonies, and Trade.Cambridge University Press.*

Aubet, M.E. (2001). *The Phoenicians and the West.* Cambridge University Press.

Bagnall, N. (1999). *The Punic Wars: Rome, Carthage and the Struggle for the Mediterranean.* London: Pimlico.

Bath, T. (1995). *Hannibal's Campaigns. New York: Barnes & Noble Books.*

Bondi, S.F. (2001). Political and Administrative Organization. *The Phoenicians* (S. Moscati, Ed.). London: I.B. Tauris.

Carthage. Encyclopedia Britannica. (1998, July 20). https://www.britannica.com/place/Carthage-ancient-city-Tunisia

Cartwright, M. (2016, April 28). *The Phoencians – Master Mariners*. World History. https://www.worldhistory.org/article/897/the-phoenicians---master-mariners/

Champion, J. (2017). *Pyrrhus of Epirus*. Pen and Sword Press.

Coulmas, F. (1996). The Blackwell Encyclopedia of Writing Systems. Oxford: Blackwell.

Dietler, M. & C. López-Ruiz (2009). *Colonial Encounters in Ancient Iberia: Phoenician, Greek, and Indigenous Relations* by M, University of Chicago Press.

Drummond, A. (2012). Atilius Regulus, Marcus. The Oxford Classical Dictionary (4th ed.) (S. Hornblower et al., Ed.). Oxford University Press.

Eckstein, A. (2017). The First Punic War and After, 264-237 BC. *The Encyclopedia of Ancient Battles* (pp. 1-14).

Emery. K.P. (2016). Carthaginian Mercenaries: Soldiers of Fortune, Allied Conscripts, and Multi-Ethnic Armies in Antiquity. Digital Commons @ Wofford College. https://digitalcommons.wofford.edu/studentpubs/11

Fantar, M.H. (2000). Were living Children Sacrificed to the Gods? No. *Archaeology Odyssey*.

Frahm, E. (2017). *The Neo-Assyrian Period (ca. 1000–609 BCE). A Companion to Assyria (E. Frahm, Ed.). Hoboken: John Wiley & Sons.*

Freeman, P.M. (2010). Ancient references to Tartessos. *Celtic from the West* (B. Cunliffe & J.T. Koch, Eds.). Havertown: Casemate.

Goldsworthy, A. (2008). *The Fall of Carthage: The Punic Wars 265-146 BC*. London: Orion.

Head, B., et al. (1911). Zeugitana. *Historia Numorum* (2nd ed.) (pp. 877-882). Oxford: Clarendon Press.

Heilbrunn Timeline of Art History: The Phoenicians (1500–300 BCE). (2000). The Met. http://www.metmuseum.org/toah/hd/phoe/hd_phoe.htm

Hieron II. (1998, July 20). Encyclopedia Britannica. https://www.britannica.com/biography/Hieron-II.

Higgins, A. (2005). Carthage tries to live down image as site of infanticide. Post Gazette.

Horstead, W. (2021). *The Numidians 300 BC–AD 300. Bloomsbury Publishing.*

Hoyos, D. (2001). Identifying Hamilcar Barca's Heights of Heircte. *Historia: Zeitschrift für Alte Geschichte,* (H. 4) (pp.490-495).

Hoyos, D. (2007). *Truceless War: Carthage's Fight for Survival, 241 to 237 BCE* Boston: Brill.

Hoyos, D. (2008). *Hannibal:Rome's greatest enemy. Exeter: Bristol Phoenix Press.*

Lancel, S. (1997). *Carthage: A History.* Oxford: Blackwell.

Lancel, S. (1999). *Hannibal.* London: Wiley-Blackwell.

Lanning, M. (2002). *The Military 100: A Ranking of the Most Influential Leaders of All Time.* Citadel Press.

Law, R.C.C. (1978). North Africa in the period of Phoenician and Greek colonization, c. 800 to 325 BC. *The Cambridge History of Africa* Vol. 2 (Fage & R.A. Oliver, Eds.). Cambridge University Press.

Lazenby, J.F. (1996). *The First Punic War: a Military History* (pp. 145-148). London: UCL Press.

Markoe, G.E. *Phoenicians (Peoples of the Past Series).* Berkeley: University of California Press.

Matyszak, P. (2009). *The Enemies of Rome.* London: Thames & Hudson.

Miles, R. (2010). *Carthage Must Be Destroyed: The Rise and Fall of an Ancient Civilization.* Allen Lane.

Relics of Carthage show brutality amid the good life. (1987, September 1). *The New York Times.*

Roger, S.R. (2004). A History of Writing. Reaktion Books.

St. Clair, K. (2016). *The Secret Lives of Colour (pp. 162-164). London: John Murray.*

Stieglitz, R. (1990). *The Geopolitics of the Phoenician Littoral in the Early Iron Age. Bulletin of the American Schools of Oriental Research, 129(9).*

The Phoenicians: A Captivating Guide to the History of Phoenicia and the Impact Made by

One of the Greatest Trading Civilizations of the Ancient World. (2019). Captivating History.

Utica. (1998, July 20). Encyclopedia Britannica. https://www.britannica.com/place/Utica-Tunisia

Walbank, F.W. (1957). *A Historical Commentary on Polybius. Vol. 1. Oxford: Clarendon Press.*